KATHLEEN JAMIE

The Queen of Sheba

BLOODAXE BOOKS

ISBN: 1 85224 284 1

First published 1994 by
Bloodaxe Books Ltd,
P.O. Box 1SN,
Newcastle upon Tyne NE99 1SN.

Bloodaxe Books Ltd acknowledges
the financial assistance of Northern Arts.

Cover printing by J. Thomson Colour Printers Ltd, Glasgow.

Printed in Great Britain by
Bell & Bain Limited, Glasgow, Scotland.

THE QUEEN OF SHEBA

Also by Kathleen Jamie

POETRY

Black Spiders (Salamander Press, 1981)
A Flame in Your Heart, with Andrew Greig
 (Bloodaxe Books, 1986)
The Way We Live (Bloodaxe Books, 1987)
The Autonomous Region, with Sean Mayne Smith
 (Bloodaxe Books, 1993)

TRAVEL

The Golden Peak (Virago, 1992)

This one's for the folks at home

Acknowledgements

Acknowledgements are due to the editors of the following publications in which some of these poems first appeared: *Chapman, The Best of Scottish Poetry* (Chambers, 1989), *Dream State: The New Scottish Poets* (Polygon, 1994), *Gairfish, The New Poetry* (Bloodaxe Books, 1993), *New Statesman & Society, The Observer Magazine, Pequod* (USA), *Poetry Review, Poetry with an Edge* (Bloodaxe Books, new edition, 1993), *The Printer's Devil, Rubicon* (Canada), *The Scotsman, Sixty Women Poets* (Bloodaxe Books, 1993), *The Times Literary Supplement* and *Verse*.

'Child with pillar box and bin bags' was read on *Stanza* (BBC Radio 4). Kathleen Jamie's version of 'In Praise of Aphrodite' was commissioned by the South Bank Centre as part of the celebrations of Tsvetayeva's centenary. 'Mr and Mrs Scotland are dead' won third prize in the 1993 National Poetry Competition.

Contents

The Queen of Sheba

Scotland, you have invoked her name
just once too often
in your Presbyterian living rooms.
She's heard, yea
even unto heathenish Arabia
your vixen's bark of poverty, come down
the family like a lang neb, a thrawn streak,
a wally dug you never liked
but can't get shot of.

She's had enough. She's come.
Whit, tae this dump? Yes!
She rides first camel
of a swaying caravan
from her desert sands
to the peat and bracken
of the Pentland hills
across the fit-ba pitch
to the thin mirage
of the swings and chute; scattered with glass.

Breathe that steamy musk
on the Curriehill Road, not mutton-shanks
boiled for broth, nor the chlorine stink
of the swimming pool where skinny girls
accuse each other of verrucas.
In her bathhouses women bear
warm pot-bellied terracotta pitchers
on their laughing hips.
All that she desires, whatever she asks
She will make the bottled dreams
of your wee lasses
look like *sweeties*.

Spangles scarcely cover
her gorgeous breasts, hanging gardens
jewels, frankincense; more voluptuous
even than Vi-next-door, whose
high-heeled slippers

keeked from dressing gowns
like little hooves, wee tails
of pink fur stuffed in the cleavage of her toes;
more audatious even than Currie Liz
who led the gala floats
through the Wimpey scheme
in a ruby-red Lotus Elan
before the Boys' Brigade band
and the Brownies' borrowed coal-truck;
hair piled like candy-floss;
who lifted her hands fom the neat wheel
to tinkle her fingers
at her tricks
        among the Masons and the elders and the police.

The cool black skin
of the Bible couldn't hold her,
nor the atlas green
on the kitchen table,
you stuck with thumbs
and split to fruity hemispheres –
yellow Yemen, Red Sea, *Ethiopia*. Stick in
with the homework and you'll be
cliver like yer faither.
but no too cliver,
no *above yersel.*

See her lead those great soft camels
widdershins round the kirk-yaird,
smiling
as she eats
avocados with apostle spoons
she'll teach us how. But first

she wants to strip the willow
she desires the keys
        to the National Library
she is beckoning
    the lasses
        in the awestruck crowd...

Yes, we'd like to
          clap the camels,
to smell the spice,
admire her hairy legs and
bonny wicked smile, we want to take
PhDs in Persian, be vice
to her president: we want
to help her
          ask some Difficult Questions

she's shouting for our wisest man
to test her mettle:

          Scour Scotland for a Solomon!

Sure enough: from the back of the crowd
someone growls:
                    whae do you think y'ur?

and a thousand laughing girls and she
draw our hot breath
                    and shout:

THE QUEEN OF SHEBA!

Mother-May-I

Mother-May-I
go down the bottom of the lane,
to the yellow-headed piss-the-beds,
and hunker at the may-hedge, skirts
fanned out
   in the dirt and see the dump
where we're not allowed –
twisty trees, the burn, and say:
 all hushed sweetie-breath:
 they are the woods
where men
   lift up your skirt
and take down your pants
even although you're crying.
Mother may I
   leave these lasses' games
    and play at Man-hunt, just
in the scheme Mother
may I
 tell small lies: *we were sot*
in the lane, sat on garage ramps,
picking harling
with bitten nails, as myths
rose thick as swamp mist
from the woods behind the dump
    where hitch-hikers rot
in the curling roots of trees,
and men
leave tight rolled-up
dirty magazines.
Mother may we

   pull our soft backsides
through the jagged may's
white blossom, run across the stinky dump
and muck about
at the woods and burn
     dead pleased
to see the white dye
of our gym-rubbers seep downstream?

A shoe

On the dry sand of Cramond I found
        a huge
                platform sole, a wedge
of rubber gateau among the o-so
rounded pebbles
            the occasional
washed up san-pro.

I could arrange it in the bathroom
with the pretty
            Queeny shells, God,
we'd laugh, wouldn't we, girls?

            Those bloody bells
ringing down corridors
hauling us this way and that;
    wee sisters and pals
        tugging our hair,
            folders, books
and those shoes – stupid
as a moon walker's; ah,
            the comfort of gravity.

You don't suppose she just
            stepped off the Forth Bridge,
head over heels, shoes self-righting
            like a cat,
hair and arms flying up
    as she slid down through the water?

Or did she walk in, saying yes
            I recognise this
as the water yanked heavy
    on thighs belly breasts?

God girls, we'd laugh:
            it's all right once you're in.
it's all right
            once you're out the other side.

Hand relief

Whatever happened to friends like Liz,
who curled her legs on a leather settee,
and touched your knee, girl/girl,
as she whispered what the businessmen of Edinburgh
wear beneath their suits –

laughed and hooked her hair back
saying Tuesday, giving some bloke
hand relief, she'd looked up at the ceiling
for the hundredth time that lunch-hour,
and screaming, slammed the other hand down hard
on the panic button; had to stand there
topless in front of the bouncers
and the furious punter, saying
sorry, I'm sorry, it was just a spider...

Whatever happens to girls like Liz
fresh out of school, at noon on a Saturday
waiting for her shift at Hotspots
sauna, in a dressing gown
with a pink printed bunny
who follows you to the window
as you look out at the city
and calls you her pal. She says, *you're a real pal.*

Child with pillar box and bin bags

But it was the shadowed street-side she chose
while Victor Gold the bookies basked
in conquered sunlight, and though
Dalry Road Licensed Grocer gloried and cast
fascinating shadows she chose
the side dark in the shade of tenements;
that corner where Universal Stores' (closed
for modernisation) blank hoarding blocked
her view as if that process were illegal;
she chose to photograph her baby here,
the corner with the pillar box.
In his buggy, which she swung to face her.
She took four steps back, but
the baby in his buggy rolled toward the kerb.
She crossed the ground in no time
it was fearful as Niagara,
she ran to put the brake on, and returned
to lift the camera, a cheap one.
The tenements of Caledonian Place neither
watched nor looked away, they are friendly buildings.
The traffic ground, the buildings shook, the baby breathed
and maybe gurgled at his mother as she
smiled to make him smile in his picture;
which she took on the kerb in the shadowed corner,
beside the post-box, under tenements, before
the bin-bags hot in the sun that shone
on them, on dogs, on people on the other side
the other side of the street to that she'd chosen,
if she'd chosen or thought it possible to choose.

Crystal set

Just as the stars appear, father
carries from his garden shed
a crystal set, built
as per instructions
in the *Amateur Mechanic*.
Mother dries her hands. Their boy
and ginger cat lie beside the fire.
He's reading – what – *Treasure Island*
but jumps to clear the dresser. Hush,
they tell each other. Hush!

The silly baby bangs her spoon
as they lean in to radio-waves
which lap, the boy imagines,
just like Scarborough. Indeed,
it *is* the sea they hear as though
the brown box were a shell. Dad
sorts through fizz, until, like diamonds
lost in dust – '*Listen, Ships' Morse!*' –
and the boy grips his chair. As though
he'd risen sudden as an angel
to gaze down, he understands
that not his house, not
Scarborough Beach, but the whole
Island of Britain
is washed by dark waves. Hush
they tell each other. Hush.

There is nothing to tune to
but Greenwich pips
and the anxious signalling
of ships that nudge our shores.
Dumb silent waves. But that
was then. Now, gentle listener,
it's time to take our leave
of Mum and Dad's proud glow, the boy's
uncertain smile. Besides,
the baby's asleep.
So let's tune-out here
and slip along the dial. *Hush.*

Fountain

What are we doing when we toss a coin,
just a 5p-piece into the shallow dish
of the fountain in the city-centre
shopping arcade? We look down
the hand-rail of the escalator
through two-three inches of water
at a scatter of coins: round, flat, worthless,
reflections of perspex foliage
and a neon sign – FOUNTAIN.
So we glide from mezzanine to ground,
laden with prams, and bags printed
Athena, Argos, Olympus; thinking: now
in Arcadia est I'll besport myself
at the water's edge with kids,
coffee in a polystyrene cup.
We know it's all false: no artesian well
really leaps through strata
fathoms under *Man at C&A*, but
who these days can thrust her wrists
into a giggling hillside spring
above some ancient city?
So we flick in coins, show the children how:
make a wish! What for, in the shopping mall?
A wee stroke of luck? A something else, a nod
toward a goddess we almost sense
in the verdant plastic? Who says
we can't respond; don't still feel,
as it were, the dowser's twitch
up through the twin handles of the buggy.

Royal Family Doulton

My ladies of the dark oak dresser
I reached for you above the pewter
teapots ribbed like cockles, snaps
taken with the first family Kodak
six months ago when we were wee.

Figurines in mufflers, *Top o' the hill,*
Katherine, ermine, *Demure*'s eyes
lowered in a poke bonnet; I remember
your petticoats, flower baskets,
the delicacy of gloves.

Not my Nana scrubbing floors, her fine mantle
a gas-light's; the shared lavvy, my hand
in her rough fist past the blacked-out
stair-head window no one bothered
to scrape clean, to welcome a dull sun

twenty years since the bombs.
The Doultons' heart-shaped faces
gazed at summer Downs, sparkly ballrooms.
Seized in coy pirouettes, little victims
of enchantment, the tenement was condemned.

Handed down. On the mattresses
of my various floors I saw you trip
along lanes, hold tiny parasols
against the glare of naked bulbs,
peek behind fans in a house

where shaven-haired women
slept in the same bed,
and Jim greased guns for burial
in a revolutionary field.
One day I smothered them

in bubble-wrap, like a mother
I read of who smothered her kids
for fear of the Bomb,
took them back to the safety
of my parents' built-in wardrobe,

in case they got smashed,
little arms and bonnets, parasols
and scattered baskets. One day, I said
I'll have a calm house, a home
suitable for idols; but it hasn't happened yet.

School reunion

1

We were always the first to get snow
up here in the hills, sagging on roofs
like a shirt tail
        laying on the dreels
rich brown before they built more houses.

It's time. Taxis crunch the gravel
        at the Kestrel Hotel, its fake
coach-lamps shine yellow.
            Come in, we're
                almost
                   all here.

Downstairs, women
who work in banks are dancing, handbags
piled like ashes at their feet.

They raise their arms
in the disco lights, bra straps droop.
those faces turn, eyes, the same
lipstick mouths...
        In the Ladies/
            Girls

A glass vase & twist of plastic fuchsia.
      Laughter   Hairspray
        holds   the air
smiles stale
          fag ash   grey
cubicle doors clang; my shoes are wrong
                the tongue
                shocks with blood
                fuck off you
a pin scratches:

I want McKean
to shag me – Gemma
        is a bitch whore slag tart
                        Our voices
rise and rise, breasts fall
        toward pink-pastel basins,
            as we take out lipsticks, lean
into mirrors   look   our mother's faces
            rise to greet us
        framed in paper rosebuds
        from the opposite wall.

2

The child birls in the frosty playground,
her woolly hat, gloves flying on strings.

The text of a dream: wild earth
                        carpet
emulsion in peach blossom.
            Decree Nisi, two years
    South Australia;
                        we have
                        almost all come back

the D.J. who lived down the lane,

Linda   willowy acrobat
divorce   cartwheels, skirts
Expecting   (again)   cover her face

        a mother's grip
    *can't you be more
        ladylike*,   women
                            beware
                            gravity.

Lorraine Paton   (she's started
Gillian   she's started
that Michelle   She started and all

ganging up, the fruity weight of a gang
swaying slowly, ganging up.
                                        You!

                    snot-bag
        Ya: Fat boy, Lezzie
    ya spaz, gowk, snobby get, ya poofter

that Sandra

we knew each other utterly, the spinning bairn

                            ya lying cow she never
            threw herself under a train

    The grey clanging metal lavvy doors.

3

Oh who
                is that: gliding between darkened tables
                turquoise and gold strap, tropical blackhair
                on a bare arm tiny
                diamond in her slender nose o who
                            in the disco-lights...
                Couldn't I have dared to be
                Hazel Thompson, the weight of all hair
                lists her head as though she hears
                birdsong in Africa
                through the stamping disco
                tilts as the diamond
                tugs toward its black mine
                hair grown since we were
                seven   secret as marijuana
                in her dad's shed
                            their council house maroon door.
                I'd like to
                gather up that black hair
                Clarks shoes slapping
                down the street straight and grey
                as a school skirt, rainwater stains
                on harled gables, NO BALL GAMES

to see her in turquoise and gold
give it her in armfuls, Hazel
witchy
sweet as a   *wait, let me*
                                chum you...
Oh who   would have thought it?

4

When we're older than a mattress
on the dump, and shudder
in the living rooms of daughters
who're 60, who put on lipstick and
kindly lead us out
                to lunch in cold hotels
        that smell of paint, specimen
vases with plastic fuchsias
                and our shoes are wrong, shuffling on the red carpet,
        again we'll enter The Kestrel Hotel's
dim loud dance hall;
                as diners turn in the cool light,
mouth open, those appalled young eyes;
        we know whose names we will mutter & shout
                        we are almost all here
as our daughters hush us.

5

The first snow. Taxis turn
onto the high road,
the Wimpey scheme's
familiar streets. Distant lights
flash calmly
on the Forth Bridge, warning aircraft.

                        The morning after, waking
                        in your parents' too-small house,
                        the single bed, & wardrobe
                        brought from Granny's when she died

                              Today we'll take a walk
                              flat shoes, damp stains
                              on the harled gables;
                              to the fields; perhaps
                              a kestrel
                                        hovering still above the road.

Our laughter sealed in taxis, those faces
turn, eyes, same lipstick mouths;
goodbyes   your corner
with the privet hedge whose leaves
like greasy silk you pulled
one by one, under the streetlamp.

                    In yellow light, the bairn spins

a coloured twist
within us, like a marble.
                              Close the taxi door and wave
know we are the space
the others ease into
at your old road-end.

The taxi lights recede through the scheme's
dour streets   You watch
          from the same door,
                    then let yourself in.

As if
it's never happened
          all that's happened since.

Bairns of Suzie: a hex

Have you not seen us, the Bairns of Suzie
under the pylons of Ormiston Brae
running easy
      with foxes and dogs, high
on the green hill, high
      in the luke-warm mother's glance
of midwinter sun?

Have you not seen us
      in the rustling whin,
         the black
Gioconda smile of the broom pods?

      Ablow the pine-tree
where a nylon rope
swings from a strong limb?

      Children of Suzie come out to play
on the stone nipple
of the Black Craig

         open-leggèd, chuckling
as Vorlich and Shiehallion
snow-rise across the wide Tay,

    laughing like jackdaws as we peel
      skinny scratches of bramble
      from our inner arms
roll them like cigarettes
between our twig fingers,
         tip them
with jags from the dog-rose
tangled
      in the hair-nests
of each other's armpits and sex:

    fast
    invisible arrows, hexed
          for you

with your laws and guns,
                who'd take this hill,
shake in the people's faces keys
to courtrooms and gates
                the arrows
will enter like stars
find you
staring at the ceiling of your too-hot
                        todd-reeking rooms
night after night

until, whey-faced and desperate
you look for culprits
on the dour pavements you'd have us walk
                nose to tail
looking for Bairns of Suzie
among the wifes in scarfs,
the prams at the Co-op door the old boys'
grey-muzzled dogs
by the sunny bench at the mill.

But they will shake their douce heads,
                old seed heads
the keys of larch and rowan berries shaking
and point in different directions
each to their own home,

to the very stones of their homes,
the lintels, thexstanes, hearth
warning that such a red stone
could have come only
from the Abbey and the Grand Castle
ruined utterly
                at the town's edge.

And the Bairns of the witch of this hill
run on, loose limbed & laughing.

Boy in a blanket

Frost had crept to the river
like deer: cold vapour rose
as we crossed by a split log

to the burning-place:
bells and tiny cymbals
winked like planets in the ash. But, ah,

wasn't everything pristine –
hills, river, a crimson-breasted bullfinch
cupped in a stark tree,

and the inn-keeper's boy,
crazy as a staircase,
shouted his few words of our language

from the family's home-made
verandah, fruit trees
shrunk back to a stone.

So too the next valley;
a 'herd combing the long hair
of his goats

showed us a spring: rags
of clothing rotted on twigs.
Downstream: a rope bridge,

a creaking mill, the house on stilts
of menstruating women
heavy with vines:

and girls, pipes tucked
in their belts
watched as we climbed the inn's stairs.

To work fast, before winter –
before the barefoot boy
in a blanket who'd followed us

put them to fright, and the bells
combs, reed-pipes, harvest songs,
and bright dresses

were hid in blackened rafters
or buried like seeds,
dormant till they imagined we'd gone.

Wee Baby

In a dark and private place –
                    your handbag
she knits herself existence.
She sums and divides herself
from half-forgotten phone numbers.

She has slavered on the future
pages of your diary
to make
        a papier-mâché baby
she rubs herself with lipstick,

renders herself visible,
because she only just exists, like a stamp hinge.

She sticks. She dangles from her fathers.
She turns little fishy tricks
in your wine glass: you swallow,
now:
        open your mouth and who cries out?

Wee Baby's come to work:
she is tucked up in the in-tray.
Wee Baby's in the kitchen:
she is cradled in the sieve of all potential.

She blows about the desert in a sand-pram,
O traveller. And driver –
who flashes so indignant
on the outside lane?

She's on the town tonight, she's giving her first smile,
she's playing with her toes
on a high and lonely bar-stool.
You know you're thirty, and she loves you.

The kingdom of Wee Baby is within.
She curls her fists and holds tight.

Wee Wifey

I have a demon and her name is
>WEE WIFEY

I caught her in a demon trap – the household of my skull
I pinched her by her heel throughout her wily transformations
until
>she confessed
>>her name indeed to be WEE WIFEY

and she was out to do me ill.

So I made great gestures like Jehovah: dividing
land from sea, sea from sky,
>my own self from WEE WIFEY

(*There*, she says, *that's tidy!*)

Now I watch her like a dolly
keep an eye,
>and mourn her:

For she and I are angry/cry
>because we love each other dearly.

It's sad to note
>that without
>>WEE WIFEY

I shall live long and lonely as a tossing cork.

Outreach

With a stick in the hot dust
I draw a tenement, a plane, a church:
my country we have no
family fields. In a smoke-choked hut
where a barren wife gave birth
they pat the sackcloth, *sit!*
while hens peck round the sleeping kids
and someone coughs, coughs. *What your family?*

Hunkered in the mean shade
of our compound walls: *Your tits
not big!* Our yard grows
nothing, their constant feet.
At noon, the murderous heat,
I clang the gate: *come back tomorrow.*
Perhaps in my heart of hearts
I lack compassion. I lie

hot nights on a straight bed,
watch crowded stars through mosquito mesh
and talk to Jesus. Moonlight
strikes our metal gate like a silent gong.
Sometimes I wake
to a dog's yelp, a screech of owl,
sometimes, a wide-eyed girl
hugely wrapped in shawls. *What your husband?*

I walk a fine line with the headman,
write home: *One day I'll build a church*;
because I believe in these Lazarus' huts
are secret believers;
and listen in village lanes
of bones and dung for Jesus' name
among the shouts, the bleating goats,
the bursts of dirty laughter.

Coupie

I remember also, a stain we ignored
till it moved its thin monument of legs
and we stood either side of a head
pillowed in mud;
the tender wool of the throat.

Those day-glutted, yellow-tinged eyes,
salty as mussels; the blue black
beaks of ravens. I remember
that hopeless pedalling;
the wool grease up to my wrists

as we hauled, that last winter
before we left for different countries.
I remember: the coupie's
straw-eyed stare of complicity
when I glanced back.

China for lovers

Darling, we're in China;
a bus station motel. Do you feel
your sweat mix with noodle-steam
and diesel? What place

I can't tell. Our map was nicked
by a sneak-thief in the market square.
Perhaps their need
was desperate. We're at least aware

that we're someplace in China.
So let's quit this rucked grey sheet,
and step into the midsummer midnight heat
of a balcony

that's lost its grip.
As the town clock chimes out
twelve, thirteen, let me whisper:
deep in China means

if something normal
like a telephone's ring
reaches us over the vile latrine,
the barking mongrels, the lost sheep,

the all-night mechanic's metallic beats,
it is not for us. Not once
in the lives of girls asleep
in cauliflower trucks

or their fathers', who in blue serge suits
play cards by gaslight on an upturned box
are our names mentioned.
Now, come back indoors

and take it slow. Who's to know?
Who's to care if a quilt slithers
from a hard bed to a dusty floor,
darling, somewhere in China.

Perfect day

I am just a woman of the shore
wearing your coat against the snow
that falls on the oyster-catchers' tracks
and on our own; falls
on the still grey waters
of Loch Morar, and on our shoulders
gentle as restraint: a perfect weight
of snow as tree-boughs
and fences bear against a loaded sky:
one flake more, they'd break.

All washed up

We're all washed up. The salt touch
of your lover/sculpture shape
is rockpool, wood; the armpits' jug, its weed.
I'm run aground. Crude
metaphor but all I reach,
and do I reach. Your arms drown,
though you have it in your hands
to love and sculpt. But the city we're cast up
is far from shore, far from any shore.

In Praise of Aphrodite
(after Marina Tsvetayeva)

These are wicked days. The very gods,
brought low, fold their wings
like gulls or cushie-doos

white and rain-grey. No honeyed quaich
transforms your sweat;
your low mouth's crowded

where kingdoms flutter,
stoop, take sup from your hands,
your breasts rounded as clouds.

Every flower of the cliff,
saxifrage, thrift, witch-wife:
shows your face. Your body of stone

rising, always rising armless
from the foam, whence we crawl
through salt, sweat, the white spume.

Mr and Mrs Scotland are dead

On the civic amenity landfill site,
the coup, the dump beyond the cemetery
and the 30-mile-an-hour sign, her stiff
old ladies' bags, open mouthed, spew
postcards sent from small Scots towns
in 1960: Peebles, Largs, the rock-gardens
of Carnoustie, tinted in the dirt.
Mr and Mrs Scotland, here is the hand you were dealt:
fair but cool, showery but nevertheless,
Jean asks kindly; the lovely scenery;
in careful school-room script –
The Beltane Queen was crowned today.
But Mr and Mrs Scotland are dead.

Couldn't he have burned them? Released
in a grey curl of smoke
this pattern for a cable knit? Or this:
tossed between a toppled fridge
and sweet-stinking anorak: *Dictionary for Mothers*
M:– Milk, *the woman who worries...*;
And here, Mr Scotland's John Bull Puncture Repair Kit;
those days when he knew intimately
the thin roads of his country, hedgerows
hanged with small black brambles' hearts;
and here, for God's sake, his last few joiners' tools,
SCOTLAND, SCOTLAND, stamped on their tired handles.

Do we take them? Before the bulldozer comes
to make more room, to shove aside
his shaving brush, her button tin.
Do we save this toolbox, these old-fashioned views
addressed, after all, to Mr and Mrs Scotland?
Should we reach and take them? And then?
Forget them, till that person enters
our silent house, begins to open
to the light our kitchen drawers,
and performs for us this perfunctory rite:
the sweeping up, the turning out.

Flashing green man

I regret the little time I make to consider
these adult days, as you take a photo
to the window, tilt it to the winter light.
Now I'm one of the city. Under the multi's
walking tall and bejewelled
across our dark land, I wait with the others:
thinking about supper and the grocer's wife,
whom he said, as he weighed out potatoes,
had been mugged. But these days I don't much consider.

The green man flashed – he too refuged in cities –
and the traffic stilled for the shouting
news-vendor in his cap and scarf, for us
blethering people; and a sound
in the orange glow: a high *kronk-honk*
that made me picture those ancient contraptions
abandoned on farms. But I stopped
on the rush hour pavement to watch
the skein's arrow
cross the traffic-choked Marketgait,
and head for the glittering multi's
tenth or twelfth floor, where they banked
in the wind of these pivotal buildings
to pull themselves North to the Sidlaws:
and brash light from windows
where clerks tugged on street clothes,
coated their wings in silver and gold;
and people flowed round me
intent on home; from the roundabout's hub
traffic wheeled off to the suburbs.

If not them, perhaps someone high in the multi's –
say a pale-faced woman peeling potatoes
as her husband climbed the long stairs,
listened, smiled, and wiping the window
cupped her hands round her eyes
to acknowledge a sign
truer than the flashing green man

or directional arrows below at a junction
where I watched the geese tilt
to make their turn, their beating wings
more precious than angels' in the city lights.

Arraheids

See thon raws o flint arraheids
in oor gret museums o antiquities
awful grand in Embro –
Dae'ye near'n daur wunner at wur histrie?
Weel then, Bewaur!
The museums of Scotland are wrang.
They urnae arraheids
but a show o grannies' tongues,
the hard tongues o grannies
aa deid an gaun
back to thur peat and burns,
but for thur sherp
chert tongues, that lee
fur generations in the land
like wicked cherms, that lee
aa douce in the glessy cases in the gloom
o oor museums, an
they arenae lettin oan. But if you daur
sorn aboot an fancy
the vanished hunter, the wise deer runnin on;
wheesht … an you'll hear them,
fur they cannae keep fae muttering
ye arenae here tae wonder,
whae dae ye think ye ur?

Den of the old men

C'mon ye auld buggers, one by one
this first spring day, slowly down
the back braes with your walking sticks
and wee brown dugs, saying: *Aye, lass
a snell wind yet but braw.* Ye
half dozen relics of strong men
sat in kitchen chairs
behind the green gingham curtain
of yer den, where a wee dog grins
on last year's calendar – we hear ye
clacking dominoes the afternoon for pennies.
And if some wee tyke
puts a chuckie through the window
ye stuff yesterday's Courier
in the broken pane, saying
jail's too guid fur them, tellies in cells!
        We can see your bunnets nod
and jaws move: what're ye up to
now you've your hut built,
now green hame-hammered benches
appear in the parish's secret soft-spots
like old men's spoor?
Is it carties? A tree-hoose?
Or will ye drag up driftwood;
and when she's busy with the bairns
remove your daughters' washing-lines
to lash a raft? Which,
if ye don't all fall out and argue
you can name the *Pride o' Tay* and launch
some bright blue morning on the ebb-tide
and sail away, the lot of yez,
staring straight ahead
                like captains
as you grow tiny
out on the wide Firth, tiny
as you drift past Ballinbriech, Balmurnie, Flisk
with your raincoats and bunnets,
                wee dugs and sticks.

Jocky in the wilderness

Jock, away and tell it to the bees:
they're closing down the factory.
The Post Office women say:
is that old Jock? we thocht he was deid!
If Jocky's deid, who's dossing
in the derelict biggin
at Hazleton Wa's? The slates
are flown, the sternies prick like whin.
Whose pink trampled blanket's this,
whose fist-crushed lager tins?

Jock's a-brawling on the Aberdeen train.
I'll punch your heid! he says to his weans
I'll punch *your* heid! repeat the weans.
The shipyard roof's stripped o lead,
the bosses fled, the plant
is wede awa. At closing time
womenfolk get up and bar the door.
They're shouting through the letterbox:
Jock: enough's enough! awa

and reconstruct yourself
in your various dens; come hame
when ye've learned
to unclench your fists and hert.
So Jock walks the sheuchs
of the parish of his birth
trails of sticky-willy on his poor coat,
scares bairns in the river haar,
in their bedtime tales.
Jock-in-the-ditch are you no feart
they'll concrete over your redundant limbs?
Are you smiling with the foxes yet,
do you ken the wildflowers names?
Den of Milltown, Den of Dens, Den of Lindores.
Jocky's in the wilderness.
Jocky all alane.

One of us

We are come in a stone boat,
a miracle ship that steers itself
round skerries where guillemots
and shags stand still as graves.
Our sealskin cloaks are clasped
by a fist-sized penannular brooch,
our slippers are feathery
gugas' necks: so delicate
we carried them over the wracky shore,
past several rusted tractors. Truth:
this was a poor place, a
ragged land all worn to holes. No one,
nothing, but a distant
Telecom van, a bungalow
tied with fishing floats
for want of flowers.
                    That August night
the Perseid shower rained
on moor and lily-loch, on a frightened world –
on us, in a roofless shieling
with all our tat: the
golden horn of righteousness,
the justice harp; what folks expect.
We took swans' shape
to cross the Minch, one last fling
with silly magic – at our first
mainland steps a dormobile
slewed into a passing place; cameras flashed.
So we stayed high, surprised
a forester making aeolian flutes
from plastic tubes,
he shared his pay. 'Avoid
the A9. For God's sake,
get some proper clothes.' We ditched
the cloaks, bought yellow
Pringle sweaters in Spean Bridge,
and house by safe house
arrived in Edinburgh. So far so
tedious: we all hold
minor government jobs, lay plans, and bide our time.

Sky-burial

On the litter I tilt, sweat,
sail the day-blue
iris of sky; my eyes
flick open like a doll's.
Friends, am I heavy? You bear me
under larches in their first green,
pink nipply flowers
                    droop, tease my lips.
Iris leaves rustle, babble of streams.
Your feet seek stones, slip
the water's glassy sheen.
Level me, *steady*, your murmurs
could be   turbanned merchants
in far-flung bazaars,
my arms lashed gently to my side.

Are we there? whispers a child, no,
                    the stone trail twists
I out-stare the blind sky,
                    twin hawks
spiral the stair of their airy tower,
king & queen calling
repulsed   bound.

A heather plateau;
travelling winds bring home on their backs
scented oils,
                    rotting birds, bog-weeds.
Arenas of peat-lips
speak of forests, old wolves.
Dry lochans reveal
                    deer-spoor
creamy long-bones of trees.

Now friends, women in a ring,
raise your arms
part the blue sky

to a dark pupil; intelligent eye,
        ice-black retina of stars

slip me in.

                And if the child asks,
as you dust your hands,
turn down toward home in the green glen

                where do they go, the dead?
                Someone at last
may crack a small joke,

one say she feels watched;
one tug soft arching branches
over the burn.

You may answer him:
            here,   here,

                                            here.

Midsummer on the high moor
my eyes flick open:
                        bouquets
of purple iris, midnight
cathedrals of sky.

The wind unravels me
winter birds will arrive.

Sad Bird

A sad bird
has come to the gutter
of the house-next-door, to sit
on the dull metal rim of the rhone.
It's midnight, every other bird
is tidied away. This grey
pigeon or kind of dove hangs
its head, beak on a breast
yellowed in streetlight.
Like an ornament, it softens
the hard line the pitched
slate roof makes with sheer walls,
the house beneath: a derelict
where, daily for a whole year
two workmen, one old, one young,
arrived in a battered car.
The sad bird looks down
on a home now painted cream, pink
around windows
slightly steamed with breath,
looks sadly down
on us, standing hand in hand
on the mild street, quite still.
Perhaps it's
just resting, homing north
feeling the river and north hills,
only resting
the short night. It's we
who whisper 'sad', 'a *sad* bird',
we who feel a small grief, precise
as a drug, measured and dropped
into the bird's plain thought;
like dark that tints
the gloaming above the river
where we've just walked;
– not so much
as to be unbearable, not the dark of
winter. Above us, the bird blinks.

Above it, a silky night
which won't last long, not
too long, still, alone.

The sad bird was there again last night,
on the third night, gone.

Swallows and swifts

Twitter of swallows and swifts:
'tickets and visas, visas and tickets' –
winter, and cold rain
clears the milky-way of birdshit
where wires cross the lane.

Hagen and the owls at Glencoe

There's a touch of the witch,
a shaft of God between clouds
a death in the house, and life
is a cobweb of glass.

The cat's buried at the river,
his death weighs like water in a sack
the owls that cry in the night-time
dropped us a mouse with no back.

Such things by the door in the morning!
things to keep you knowing
that God is in the potting shed,
puts your eye to a crack between slats.

The Republic of Fife

Higher than the craw-stepped
gables of our institutes – chess-clubs,
fanciers, reels & Strathspeys –
the old kingdom of lum, with crowns agley.

All birds will be citizens: banners
of starlings; Jacobin crows – also:
Sonny Jim Aitken, Special P.C.
whose red face closed in polis cars

utters *terrible, ridiculous*
at his brother and sister citizens
but we're no feart, not of anyone
with a tartan nameplate screwed to his door.

Citizen also: the tall fellow I watched
lash his yurt to the leafy earth,
who lifted his chin
to my greeting, roared AYE!

as in YES! FOREVER! MYSELF!
The very woods where my friend Isabel
once saw a fairy, blue as a gas flame
dancing on trees. All this

close to the motorway
where a citizen has dangled,
maybe with a friend clutching
his/her ankles to spray

PAY NO POLL TAX on a flyover
near to Abernethy, in whose tea rooms
old Scots kings and bishops in mitres
supped wi a lang spoon. Citizens:

our spires and doocoots
institutes and tinkies' benders,
old Scots kings and dancing fairies
give strength to my house

on whose roof we can balance,
carefully stand and see
clear to the far off mountains,
cities, rigs and gardens,

Europe, Africa, the Forth and Tay bridges,
even dare let go, lift our hands
and wave to the waving citizens
of all those other countries.

The horse-drawn sun

We may lie forsaken in the earth's black gut,
but days are still lit, harvests annual,
skies occasionally blue.
So remember. Pay heed.

Our struggle to surface
after thousands of years is, forgive me,
to break up with a nightmare. Apposite
mate for a horse of the light?

Forget it. Were I not sacred
my work would be duller than
turning a threshing mill.
But it's nothing; an honour.

I draw strength from the burden I've hauled
like a Clydesdale through a hundred
closed generations. But what's an age?
a mere night. I sense light

near exhumation, the plough-share
tearing the earth overhead.
– Go on; blind me. Hear the whinny beneath
the tremor of sun underground. Let us out

to raise a new dawn this dull afternoon.
Let us canter high and look down.
This is the sacred horse drawing the sun.
Let's see what they've lost. What they've become.

A dream of the Dalai Lama on Skye

A summer wind blows the horn of Glen Brittle.
It's a hard walk, Black Cuillin
to his left hand; asks
the midsummer moon
setting over Canna, *what metaphors*
does the market whisper?
If the hills changed shape,
> *who would tell me?*
She shines on ditches choked
with yellow iris: butter-lamps
in a temple corner; a snail-shell
in his moonlit palm:
the golden dimple of an icon's smile.
> He smiles too, notes
the private union of burn and sea,
as one by one, laverocks rise,
irises open. When no one's watching,
he jumps lightly onto Soay
and airborne seeds
of saxifrage, settled
> on the barren Cuillin
waken into countless tiny stars.

Another day in paradise

1

You're running across the sand
of your desert island: something's
arriving. You splash into the sea,
pick it up with both hands. It's a

shoppers-survey come government-demand,
with a slight genetic spelling error:
it's addressed to someone sensible,
someone you might have been...

So: you fold it tenderly
to form a small boat
that flutters in your cupped hands
and wants to sail, but first

you place on board
a sculpture of your own creation:
island totem; an electric blue feather,
a shell, the stretched and cured

pelt of a wild-fruit,
which you wrap around a pebble
in the manner of shepherds
with an orphaned lamb.

The little boat bobs out on a turquoise sea
not to the government,
nor the council
nor the tax-collecters, none of whom can be trusted

but toward the brand shining new
state museum which
on a clear day, glints upright
like a needle just over the horizon.

They will file it in a vault.
It is one of millions. Someone
will dust them. One day
they'll stage an exhibition.

Now it is night. Noises
in the hinterland. Come dawn
you are walking, you have worn
a trench in the sand. Something is lying:

it is: a share offer/a postcard from London
a Barratt home/a ticked box;
a child's whistle blowing itself
with a scented label: Your free gift.

2

You've tied a string of yellow shells
round your ankle there is no one
to say *beautiful* or mutter *silly cow*.
You gave up gazing at the purple sea
turned inland. Didn't you know
whaups flew between palm trees,
coconuts fell to the banks
of peaty lochs with a damp thump?
Didn't you know it could rain here?
Later there became visible
a range of jagged mountains –
it's time to explore.
But because there is no one
you have written on the sand
words you thought you'd forgotten;
          forfauchlet; havers; fowk;
with the rosary of shells round your beautiful ankle
you begin to walk.

3

Following the immense curve of the glacier's spine;
you made up stories to keep yourself whole.
It was once a dragon.
You sang the songs
of your various homelands
in each of their tongues,
to the cold sky. It was easy to imagine,
jumping crevasses, you were the only person alive.
You knew the ice would blind you
like a magic silver shield in a myth.
Till then, you progressed slowly, noting
the remains of insects and birds,
looking for movement on the moraine,
and when you saw it,
knew it for trickery. All the time
you later said, I was listening
for a shepherd or his daughter
to shout from the mountainside
or play a pipe; and I dreamed they'd share
a little hard bread and some cheese,
the bread and cheese, the shout, the pipe,
so real I could smell them on the bright air.

The sea-house

In this house
are secret rotting wings,
wrecked timbers; the cupboard
under the stair
glimmers with pearl.

The sea-house
rises from dulse; salt winds
boom in its attics. Here:
my tottering
collections of shells, my ballroom
swirling with fulmars.

Morning brings
laundries of wrack,
a sea-maw's grief-shaped wing. Once
a constellation
of five pink buoys.

This place is a stranger's.
Ewers in each high room
hold a little salt water.
My musical box
is a tinkling crab.

The sea-house is purdah:
cormorants' hooked-out wings
screen every chamber. Inside
the shifting place, the
neither-nor

I knock back and forth
like the tongue of a bell
mournfully tolling
in fog, or lie
as if in a small boat
adrift in an upstairs room.

Rooms

Though I love this travelling life and yearn
like ships docked, I long
for rooms to open with my bare hands,
and there discover the wonderful, say
a ship's prow rearing, and a ladder
of rope thrown down.
Though young, I'm weary:
I'm all rooms at present, all doors
fastened against me;
but once admitted start craving
and swell for a fine, listing ocean-going prow
no man in creation can build me.

Nightwatch

The clock, with its shining hands and face
shines, fainter than a constellation,
the hours' number, the space between them.

The little glowing face and hands –
like an ordinary woman or man
who's won an unexpected prize

calmly shows the state of night
with dark hands gloved in borrowed light.
Every day that dawns

it must beg a measure, every day;
like a low-caste woman at her village well.
The poor, appeasing face and hands

spend carefully, and equally
as each hour of the night unfurls,
on sleepers, who turn their backs, like worlds.

A Sealed Room
(Gulf War, January 1992)

Prising a stone
from your own earth your fingers
wash it in a burn.
You are stopped weeping
hold it to the light:

it is a blue bead,
like a cormorant's eye
it is bright glass,
   which is molten sand
It is your own self
   huddled in a sealed room
it is a clot of oil
   that you wash and wash but cannot rid from your hands.

The Ice Queen of Ararat

My museum of birds' bones, my cold
display of butterflies, my glacier;
you came roped together in a signature
I couldn't read, stare your snowblind eyes
to the shredded clouds, the spire
where wingless creatures huddled, jumped.
The prow swings and blames
the guilty wind, while at your feet
ice-lips part, and speak
of splintered ships' holds, naves.
Curator of my gallery of white and blue,
I say: go on. Test every move with a hard staff.

At Point of Ness

The golf course shifts
uneasily beside the track
where streetlight melts
to a soft frontier with winter dark.
I cross, then, helpless as a ship,
must let night load me, before
moving on between half-sensed
dry-stane walls; day-birds tucked in some nook.

Tonight, the darkness roars.
Even the fishermen's
Nissen hut seems to breathe
beside its spawn of creels,
a dreadful beaching. I walk on,
toward the shore, where night's
split open, the entire
archipelago set as sink-weight
to the sky. A wind's

caught me now; breath frosts,
and I count, to calm me, the Sound's
lighthouses as they shine and fade
across the surge. Graemsay
beams a long systolic five
to one of dark; Hoy a distant
two: two; scattered buoys
blink where skerries drown, then cut
to sea and stars, then
bloom again, weird lilies
wilt and bloom, till,
heart-scared, I have it
understood:
>   *never*   *ever*
> *harm – this*,
>
>   *you never could*

and run – that constant roar,
the track's black vein; toward salt
lit windows, my own door...

             *

Sunshine

gleams the dry-stane dykes'
lovely melanoma of lichen. A wren
flicks on a weathered post
like a dud lighter, by the track
that splits the golf course
from the town's edge to the shore,
where I walk this afternoon
for a breath of air.

Skeins o geese

Skeins o geese write a word
across the sky. A word
struck lik a gong
afore I wis born.
The sky moves like cattle, lowin.

I'm as empty as stane, as fields
ploo'd but not sown, naked
an blin as a stane. Blin
tae the word, blin
tae a' soon but geese ca'ing.

Wire twists lik archaic script
roon a gate. The barbs
sign tae the wind as though
it was deef. The word whustles
ower high for ma senses. Awa.

No lik the past which lies
strewn aroun. Nor sudden death.
No like a lover we'll ken
an connect wi forever.
The hem of its goin drags across the sky.

Whit dae birds write on the dusk?
A word niver spoken or read.
The skeins turn hame,
on the wind's dumb moan, a soun,
maybe human, bereft.